Crochet For Beginners

The Ultimate Step by Step Guide With Picture illustrations To Learn How to Crochet. Master Your First Project In Less Than 2 Hours and Create Wonderful Projects

By

Eleanor Patel

© Copyright 2021 - All rights reserved.

This document is geared towards providing exact and reliable information in regards to the topic and issue covered. The publication is sold with the idea that the publisher is not required to render accounting, officially permitted, or otherwise, qualified services. If advice is necessary, legal or professional, a practiced individual in the profession should be ordered.

- From a Declaration of Principles which was accepted and approved equally by a Committee of the American Bar Association and a Committee of Publishers and Associations.

In no way is it legal to reproduce, duplicate, or transmit any part of this document in either electronic means or in printed format. Recording of this publication is strictly prohibited, and any storage of this document is not allowed unless with written permission from the publisher. All rights reserved.

The information provided herein is stated to be truthful and consistent, in that any liability, in terms of inattention or otherwise, by any usage or abuse of any policies, processes, or Instructions: contained within is the solitary and utter responsibility of the recipient reader. Under no circumstances will any legal responsibility or blame be held against the publisher for any reparation, damages, or monetary loss due to the information herein, either directly or indirectly.

Respective authors own all copyrights not held by the publisher.

The information herein is offered for informational purposes solely and is universal as so. The presentation of the information is without contract or any type of guarantee assurance.

The trademarks that are used are without any consent, and the publication of the trademark is without permission or backing by the trademark owner. All trademarks and brands within this book are for clarifying purposes only and are owned by the owners themselves, not affiliated with this document.

Table of Content

Introduction	7
Chapter 1: What is Crochet & its Basics	9
1.1 Crochet by Tambour	10
1.2 Crochet by Irish Famine	11
1.3 Items Yielded by Crochet	13
1.4 Yesterday & Today's Techniques	14
1.5 Patterns	15
Chapter 2: Crocheting Tools	18
2.1 Crochet Hook	18
2.2 Measuring Tools	18
2.3 Scissors	19
2.4 Tapestry Needle	20
2.5 Yarn & Gauge	20
Chapter 3: Techniques for Crocheting	23
3.1 Crochet Hooks	23
3.2 Holding a Crochet Hook	23
3.3 Making a Slip Knot	24
3.4 Crocheting a Chain Stitch	24
3.5 Single Crochet	24
3.6 Single Crochet Stitch Patterns	25
3.7 Double Crochet	25
3.8 Crochet a Granny Square	25
3.9 Make a Slip Stitch	26
3.10 Working the Basic Crochet Stitches	26

3.11 Finished Crochet	*26*
3.12 Learning Crochet Left-Handed	*26*
3.13 Check the Tension	*27*
3.14 Following a Pattern	*28*
Conclusion	*62*

Introduction

Crochet is a very flexible and popular method, and like knitting, after you master a few fundamental stitches, you can combine them to make amazing clothes and home items. Just you need is some yarn to crochet & a hook. To begin, build a basic loop (you will find it further in the book) to serve as the foundation row for all subsequent rows or rounds. Crochet stitches are formed by wrapping yarn around a hook to form loops. To form the stitches, the loops are dragged through the wrapped yarn. The chain stitches foundation may also be used to produce drawstrings or cords for knitting projects. Crochet may be used to construct both entire garments and attractive edgings for knitting. Lightweight yarns generate a delicate fabric, whereas heavier yarns provide a denser fabric, similar to knitting. Crochet is a simple skill to pick up, & your work will expand rapidly, so you'll be crafting lovely products in no time. Don't be afraid to give it a go.

Weaving, Knitting, netting, twisting, braiding, & knotting are only few of the needlework techniques that have been termed by several names throughout history. knotless netting, Needle-coiling, cross-knit looping, vatsom, looped needle-netting, Coptic knitting, nalbinding, tambour, Tunisian crochet, needle lace, lace creation, tatting, macramé, sprang, and shepherd's knitting is some of the techniques.

Hair, reeds, grasses, animal fur & sinew, hemp, wool, flax, gold and silver strands, wool yarns (soft zephyr yam, white cotton thread, luster yarn, carpet yarn), double cable yarn, cotton yarn (anchor & Estremadura), silk thread (cordonnet & floss), linen thread, mohair, hemp thread, chenille, novelty mixtures, meta

We now have a large assortment of cotton, wool, silk, and synthetic yarns at our disposal. Copper wire, plastic strips, sisal, jute, fabric scraps, unspun wool, & even dog hair are all possibilities for crocheting.

What about the crochet needle? Today, we may acquire plastic, aluminum, or steel hooks in moreover 25 sizes from a yarn store or Walmart. They utilized anything they could get their hands on in the past, including fingers, metal hooks, wood, animal bone, fishbone, horn, old spoons, comb teeth, brass, morse (walrus tusk), tortoiseshell, mother-of-pearl, ivory, copper, vulcanite, steel, ebonite, silver, and agate.

Chapter 1: What is Crochet & its Basics

Crochet is a term used by the French, Belgians, Italians, and Spanish-speaking people. In Holland, the skill was known as haken, in Denmark as haekling, in Norway as hekling, and in Sweden as virkning.

Knitting, needlework, and weaving, for example, may be traced back in time owing to archaeological findings, literary sources, and diverse graphical depictions. However, no one knows exactly when or where the crochet began. The name derives from the Center French word croc, or croche, which means hook, & the Old Norse word krokr, which means hook.

"The modern technique of real crochet as we know it now was established around the 16th century," as per American crochet expert & globe traveler Annie Potter. In France, it was known as 'crochet lace,' while in England, it was known as 'chain lace.' Walter Edmund Roth met relatives of a Guiana Indians in 1916, she says, and saw specimens of real crochet.

Lis Paludan of Denmark, another writer/researcher who focused her hunt for the roots of crochet on Europe, has three intriguing hypotheses. One: Crochet started in Arabia, traveled eastward to Tibet, then west to Spain, from which it spread to other Mediterranean nations through Arab trade routes. Two: The first evidence of crochet was found in South America, where such a primitive culture was claimed to utilize crochet adornments in puberty ceremonies. Three: Early instances of three-dimensional crochet dolls have been found in China.

However, according to Paludan, "no conclusive evidence on how ancient the technique of crochet could be and where it comes from." Crochet was almost unknown in Europe until the year 1800. "Many sources claim that crochet dates back to the 1500s in Italy when it was used by nuns for church linens under the moniker of 'nun's or 'nun's work' lace,'" she explains. Her investigation found up a number of instances of lace-making & a kind of ribbon tape, most of which have been survived, but "all indications suggest that crochet was not recognized in Italy as early as the 16th century"—under any name.

1.1 Crochet by Tambour

Crochet is said to have evolved most naturally from Chinese handiwork, a very old kind of embroidery found in Turkey, India, Persia, and North Africa that arrived in Europe in the 1700s & was dubbed "tambouring" from the French word "tambour," which means "drum." A backdrop cloth is stretched tight on a frame in this method. Underneath the cloth, a working thread is retained. A hook-tipped needle is put into the cloth & a loop of a working thread is dragged up through it. A hook then is inserted a little farther along with the loop remaining on it, & another circle of the netting is brought up & worked through the 1st loop to make a chain stitch. The tambour hook was just as tiny as a sewing needle, implying that the job was done with a very fine thread.

Tambour developed into "crochet in the air" around the end of the eighteenth century when the backdrop cloth was removed and the stitch was let to work on its own.

Crochet first appeared in Europe during the early 1800s, and Mlle gave it a huge push. Riego de Branchardiere was most recognized for her ability to convert old-fashioned needle & bobbin lace patterns into crochet patterns that could be readily replicated. She wrote a lot of pattern books enough so millions of ladies could start copying her designs. Madame. Riego also claims to be the inventor of "lace-like" crochet, which is now known as Irish crochet.

1.2 Crochet by Irish Famine

For the citizens of Ireland, Irish crochet had been a lifeline. It rescued them from a potato famine that lasted from 1845-1850 & plunged them into destitution.

The Irish had difficult living and working circumstances during this period. To take full advantage of the sunshine, they knitted in between agricultural tasks and outside. They went inside after dark to work by candlelight, a slow-burning peat fire, or an oil lamp.

Because many of them were living in filth, finding a place to store their crochet work was a challenge. If they didn't have somewhere else to put it, it went beneath the bed, where it eventually got filthy. Fortunately, the crocheted item could be cleaned and restored to its former brilliance. Ironically, purchasers in other countries were unaware that such fine collars & cuffs were produced in shacks in impoverished areas.

Crochet cooperatives were formed in Ireland, bringing together men, women, and children. Schools were established to teach the trade, and instructors were educated and sent across Ireland, where workers quickly developed their own designs. Despite the fact that over a million people perished in less than ten years, the people of Irish managed to endure the famine. Crochet earnings enabled families to save enough money to move & make a fresh start in another country, bringing their crochet abilities with them. According to Potter, two million Irish people moved to America between 1845 & 1859, and four million in 1900. American women, preoccupied with spinning, weaving, knitting, and quilting, couldn't help but be encouraged to include the crochet talents of their new neighbors into their handiwork.

a stiff wire or A needle, put into a piece of wood or tree bark or a cork, with its end filed down & curved into a small hook, was what at least one individual in Ireland used to manufacture excellent Irish crochet during the Great Famine (1845-1850).

1.3 Items Yielded by Crochet

Men - because it was their profession - developed handwork for utilitarian needs in the early ages. To capture animals and capture fish or birds, hunters and fishermen used knotted strands of ropes, woven fibers, or strips of fabric. Knotted fishing nets, game bags, and open-worked cooking utensils were among the other applications.

Personal ornamentation for special events such as religious ceremonies, festivities, weddings, and funerals was added to handwork. Ceremonial dresses may have crocheted embellishment and ornate trims on the arms, ankles, and wrists.

Royalty and the affluent in sixteenth-century Europe showered themselves in lace - trimmings, dresses, coats, and headpieces - whereas the common people could only dream of donning such garments. Crochet is said to have evolved as a poor man's copy of the wealthy man's lace.

Crochet patterns for birdcage covers, flowerpot holders, baskets for lamp mats, visiting cards, and wastepaper baskets, tablecloths, shades, antimacassars (or "antis," tends to cover to prevent chairbacks from the hair oil used by men in the middle of the 1800s), purses, tobacco pouches, men's caps & waistcoats, and even a rug with foot warmers to be placed undecorated were available in Victorian times.

Women crocheted Afghans, sleeping rugs, traveling rugs, sleigh rugs, chaise lounge rugs, vehicle rugs, cushions, coffee, and teapot cozies, & hot-water bottle covers between 1900 and 1930. Potholders first appeared about this period and quickly became a mainstay of the crocheter's repertory.

Of course, now you can do anything you want. Crochet became popular in the 1960s and 1970s as a freeform form of expression that can now be seen in three-dimensional sculptures, clothes, carpets, and tapestries depicting abstract and realistic motifs and settings.

1.4 Yesterday & Today's Techniques

It's fascinating to compare and contrast old and new crochet techniques. For example, from 1824 to 1833, the Dutch periodical Penelope noted that both yarn & the hooks were to be kept in the right hand, with the yarn being transferred over the hooks from the proper forefinger. The hook is handled within the right hand & the yarn inside the left in crochet book from the 1840s, much as right-handers use today.

It was mentioned in a German article from 1847 that one must "Keep the tension consistent, either loosely or securely crocheted; otherwise, an appealingly even texture would not be obtained. Furthermore, if you are not crocheting in a round, you must break off the yarn at the last of each row to give the crocheted item a finer finish." Thankfully, today's designs frequently teach us to work on both the right & wrong sides of the cloth we're working with. This shift occurred at the switch off the century.

The injunction to preserve the very same tension "does seem to imply the crochet hooks were from the same thickness & that the crocheter was required to work in the right tension as per the design," according to researcher Lis Paludan.

Old pattern instructions from the mid-1800s said that the hook should only be put into the rear half of the stitch and that a single crochet stitch should be used unless otherwise specified. In 1847, a European, Jenny Lambert, noted that putting the single crochet hook into the rear half of the stitch was good for producing table runners and other items, but entering the hooks through both loops can be used "for crochet sole for shoes & other products which must be thicker than usual, but the method is not suited for patterns." Unless otherwise instructed, we now automatically cycle through both loops.

1.5 Patterns

Before patterns were actually written, people would just copy the work of others. Samples were sewed onto pages in scrapbooks, sewed onto huge pieces of cloth, or stored loose in a box or bag. Author Annie Potter discovered several of these scrapbooks, which date from the late 1800s, still being used by nuns in Spain during her travels.

Crocheting various stitches together within long, thin bands - some created by adults, others started in school & added to overtime - was another method to gather stitch samples. (From 1916 until roughly 1926 in Europe, readers could purchase miniature pattern samples together with their yarn.)

The first recorded crochet designs were published in 1824.

The first colorwork crochet handbag designs were for gold & silver silk thread handbags.

Crochet books could be obtained in a variety of nations, and they were often translated through one language to another. Riego de la Branchardiere was the most well-known crochet specialist, having written over a hundred books, many of which were on crochet.

Crochet books first from the mid-nineteenth century were tiny, measuring around 4 inches to 6 inches, but they had woodcut pictures. Paludan informs us that these little gems included designs for cuffs, white lace-like collars, lace, insertions, and caps for ladies and children, as well as handbag designs for men's slippers and hats. Spool yarn (Scottish thread on spools), Cotton thread, linen, or hemp thread were advised for white crochet (insertions, matting, edgings, underwear trimming). Silk, chenille yarns &, wool, as well as gold & silver threads, were recommended for colorwork.

Modern crocheters would be enraged by those early designs, which were often inaccurate. For example, an eight-pointed star might turn out to have just six points. The reader was supposed to study the pattern yet utilize the graphic as a more precise guide, it turns out.

Chapter 2: Crocheting Tools

Crocheting requires the use of certain tools. Before you purchase, do some research on the tools to ensure you get decent equipment.

2.1 Crochet Hook

The first instrument needed is a crochet hook. Crochet designs specify the hook size to be used. This book will assist you in selecting hooks for your 1st project.

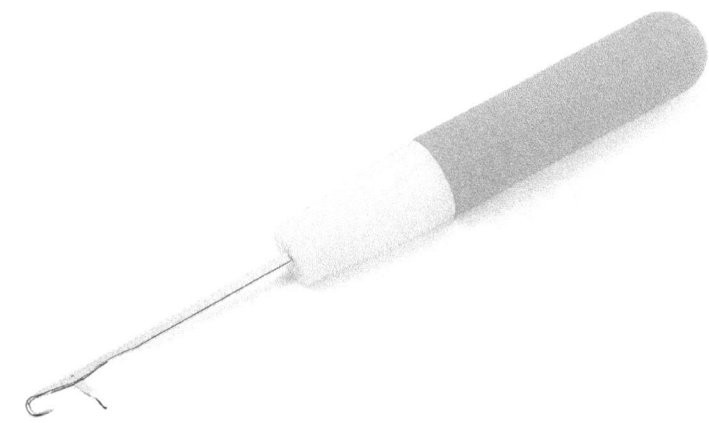

2.2 Measuring Tools

You'll need a ruler, a metal-measuring gauge, or a measuring tape to do the measurements.

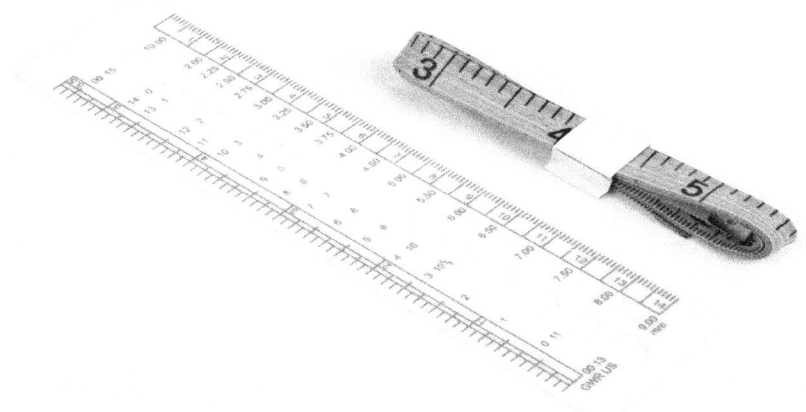

2.3 Scissors

Cut yarn, trim pompoms, and so on using shears or a tiny pair of scissors. To keep scissors safe, store them in a case.

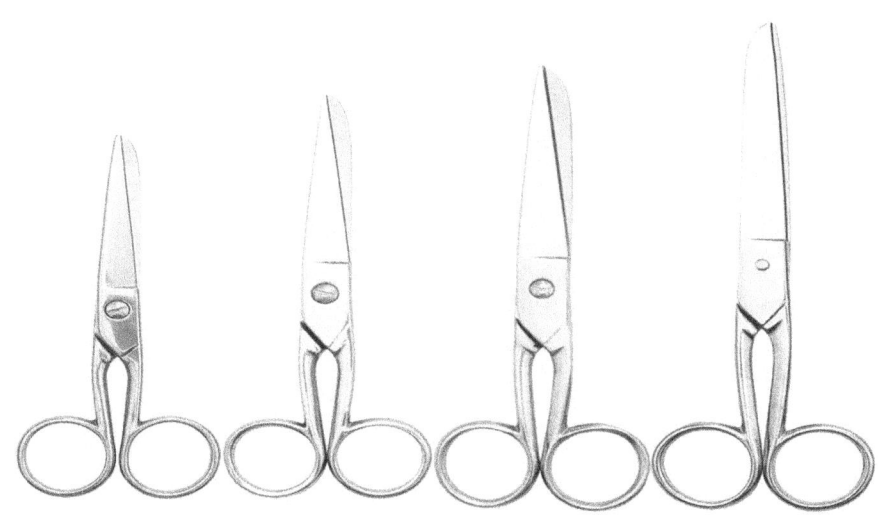

2.4 Tapestry Needle

Seams are sewn using a tapestry needle with a blunt tip. The ideal needle is a steel needle that is straight.

Around the eye of certain tapestry needles is a "hump." They're not suitable for crocheting seams since the hump snags on stitches & makes pulling the yarn through difficult.

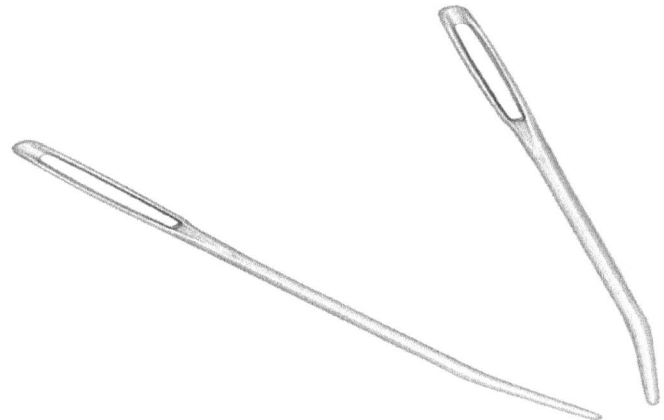

2.5 Yarn & Gauge

Yarn

Yarns come in various weights (the thickness of said strands) & fiber compositions.

Use the yarn recommended in the instructions for best results. Make careful to buy all of the yarn you'll need for the project at once since dye lots might differ slightly in shade, which will show up in the completed product. If you're working with many varieties of yarn in the same project, ensure sure they're all washed in the same way. Care instructions may be found upon the product label; carefully follow them. Always create a swatch before measuring the gauge.

Gauge

The numbers of stitches (& spaces) per inch, as well as the rows (rounds) per inch, are known as gauges. Gauge is stated over 4 inches in several designs. In order for your item to be the proper size, your gauge & the gauge indicated in the pattern should be the same. This is particularly important when working on projects which must fit together. Take your time to produce a gauge swatch before you begin your project. Use the same yarn, hook, and pattern stitch as in the instructions to verify the gauge. Make a 6-inch square swatch out of the fabric. Knit for approximately 6 inches in the pattern, then bind off. Allow the swatch to settle for a few moments before flattening it and measuring it. Mark off a piece of stitches measuring 4 inches square in the middle of the swatch using pins. In this 4 inch portion, count the amount of stitches and rows. If you match the gauges, you may begin working on your design straight away. You're knitting too loosely if you do have too few stitches; switch to a smaller hook and produce another swatch. You're working too tightly if you already have too many stitches; switch to a bigger hook. Continue to make swatches and experiment with hooks sizes until you get the desired gauge. Because everyone crochets differently, you'll be able to find a project that works for you. The yarn size and appropriate hook are listed on the label of each skein of yarn. You should preserve the label for future reference.

Crochet is also done using threads. Crochet thread is often used to make doilies, tablecloths, table toppers, and project edges. A number 10 sized thread is the most widely used thread. The fine the thread, the higher the thread number; so, 20 is better than 10, & 30 is better than 20. For this sort of crocheting, you'll need a threading hook. With such a size 10 thread, a "0" hook works perfectly.

Chapter 3: Techniques for Crocheting

Crocheting is a delicate technique that can be used to produce wonderful presents for others as well as things for your home & wardrobe. Begin by learning a few fundamental stitches, then progress to more complex basic stitches. To begin, choose the size and kind of hook that is most suitable for you. Then begin with basic yarns and basic designs, and you'll be an expert in no time.

3.1 Crochet Hooks

Crochet doesn't need a lot of materials to get started. The crochet hook is the most important component, and there are many various sizes and varieties available. If you're looking for a novice crochet hook, use one made of aluminum since the yarn will glide effortlessly. The following are the 3 basic crochet materials you'll need:

- A size H-8 or I-9 metal crochet hook, whatever feels best on your hand
- A wool yarn or ball of acrylic or skein
- Scissors

3.2 Holding a Crochet Hook

Begin by gripping your crochet hook in the same way you would a pencil, using your thumb & index finger gripping the hook at the finger hold in the center. For more comfort and control, slip your middle finger up it toward the hook's tip.

The hook will be slightly angled towards you, but not downward or upward.

3.3 Making a Slip Knot

One of the first things you'll need to learn to crochet is how to tie a slips knot onto the crochet hook. It's how you'll thread the yarn onto the hook and begin crocheting. Loop & Twist the yarn onto the hook as quickly as possible, then wrap it around the hook and draw that through the loop to tightening it. Do not worry if it seems weird at first; with practice, it will get easier.

3.4 Crocheting a Chain Stitch

The chain stitch is frequently the first stitch learned by new crocheters. Because chain stitches are the basis of most crochet items, they are among the most essential fundamental stitches to master. The shorthand for the chain stitches in a design is "ch," or "chs" for such plural form. The letter "ch" is generally associated with a number. For example, ch 135 indicates that 135 chain stitches should be crocheted.

3.5 Single Crochet

You'll learn the important single crochet stitch once you've mastered the chain stitch. The single crochet stitching can generally be abbreviated as "sc" in a design, along with the amount of stitches you will need to create.

3.6 Single Crochet Stitch Patterns

You are prepared to undertake a starting project now that you understand how to tie a slip knot & basic stitches. You might begin by crocheting a scarf or a baby blanket for beginners. For the sake of simplicity, several introductory patterns may also be written without abbreviations. Take your time and be gentle with yourself as you start your first endeavor. It's ok if you have to restart the pattern from the beginning if necessary.

3.7 Double Crochet

By mastering the double crochet stitch, you may take your crochet skills to the next level. When you master this stitch, you will be able to make Afghan granny squares. Make little swatches till your doubled crochet stitches are consistent. A double crochet stitch is abbreviated as "dc" plus the amount of the double crochet stitches provided in the design.

3.8 Crochet a Granny Square

A granny square is made out of a cluster of double crochet stitches. From blanket to pillow covers, the granny squares are the core of a crocheted items, & you can even sew these together to make a warm and snug doggy sweater. Make them one color or multicolored, but whichever color scheme you choose, know that with each square you make, you're improving as a crocheter.

3.9 Make a Slip Stitch

In crochet, slip stitches are useful for a variety of things. They may be used to link pieces together, make basic completed edges, and add a decorative element to a crocheted piece's surface. You may also use the stitches in rows to make a thick material. Bosnian Crochet is a technique for crocheting a cloth using the slip stitch (or often a variety of further names).

3.10 Working the Basic Crochet Stitches

Learn additional fundamental crochet stitches, such as the half double stitch, which generates a herringbone pattern, the treble (or triple crochet stitch), which generates a higher thread, & the Tunisian crochet stitch, which may mimic a knit fabric.

3.11 Finished Crochet

Crochet finishing methods are an essential aspect of the craft. You'll need to know how to produce broad and narrow edgings in addition to the slip stitch, which provides basic edging. A single crochet stitch is the simplest way to make an edge. Even with rounded corners, it's a fantastic option.

3.12 Learning Crochet Left-Handed

You may crochet with your left hand as well. Traditional crochet designs were intended primarily for right-handed crocheters, but so many modern designs also contain instructions for left-handed craftspeople. You'll discover lots of tips and methods to aid you along the road, & most importantly, you'll meet and learn from a lot of other lefty crocheters.

3.13 Check the Tension

Crocheting a certain size is determined by the hook size, yarn, stitch design, and you. Crochet designs provide the stitch, number of stitches, and rows necessary at the outset. Because no two individuals have the same tension, construct a trial swatch of at least 6x6 inches (15x15 cm) before beginning a project to confirm your tension matches the patterns. Your tension is too slack, and you'll need to switch to a smaller hook if your swatch has fewer stitches & rows. If you have too many, tension is too slack, and you should switch to a larger hook. Before you begin, try another sample and keep in mind that matching the numbers of stitches is typically more essential than matching the number of rows, since you may adjust for rows with working more or less to the pattern's specifications.

- Place a ruler or stiff tape all across the sample at the end of a row of stitches to measure your stitches. Place two pins 4 inches (10 cm) apart & count the stitches between them.
- Place the rulers or tapes along a column of stitches to determine row tension. Insert two pins 4 inches (10cm) apart, avoiding the edges, then count the rows in between pins.

3.14 Following a Pattern

Crochet designs are written in condensed form, similar to knitting patterns. Here's how to figure out when, where, and why to do something.

Read over the pattern before you start crocheting to make sure you know what should do in every section.

- At the conclusion of each circle, don't turn in the work.
- The turning chain is always counted as a stitch.
- In the preceding row, work into the next available stitch.
- Unless it's a loop or chain stitch, always put the hook beneath the upper loops of a stitch.
- In a pattern, the order to work 'even' implies to work without growing or decreasing.
- Asterisks are being used to indicate when a pattern is repeated in a row.
- A stitch combination is enclosed in brackets or parentheses and would be repeated in the direction indicated.

Chapter 4: Projects

4.1 Easy Crochet Scarf Pattern Using Moss Stitch

Skill: Beginner, Time: 240 Mins

The moss stitch, that is a simple stitch pattern made up of single crochet & chain stitches, is used in this simple crochet scarf design. Making single crochet threads into gaps formed by chain stitches creates the moss stitch, usually known as linen stitch or granite stitch. It just takes a few rows to master this method, which results in a lovely contemplative pattern that is perfect for beginner and experienced crochets. It's also simple enough for novices, with no rising or decreasing required. This crochet scarf design is a great way to learn and practice this lovely stitch while also making a useful and pleasant item.

Finished Measurements / Sizing

4 inches in width

Approximately 50 inches in length

Crochet scarves available in a variety of widths, so it's ok if yours is wider or narrower than the 4-inch average. If you really like the width you've achieved, no need to start again, given you purchased enough yarn. If your scarf is much fuller than 4", the most immediate thing you would have to worry about is running out of yarn.

A crochet scarf's length is easily adjustable. Do you prefer a shorter scarf? Reduce the number of rows you crochet. Is it possible to get a longer scarf? Crochet a few extra rows as long as we have yarn.

Gauge

In Moss Stitch, 14 stitches and 15 rows equal 4 inches (10 cm).

Crochet seven to ten rows of the design and measure the breadth of the item to determine your stitch gauge. Compare the initial measurement to the final measurement. If your scarf is turned out to be broader than the measurement provided, you may wish to start afresh with such a smaller crochet hook. If it's becoming too thin, you may want to start anew with a bigger crochet hook.

Abbreviations

- ch-1 sp: chain-1 space
- ch: chain
- sc: single crochet
- rep: repeat
- tch: turning chain
- st: stitch
- [ ]: repeat directives within brackets as commanded

Notes:

You will be crocheting into chains spaces in this design, which are denoted as ch-1 sp throughout the design. For temporally marking the stitch in this design, use a stitch marker, safety pin, or similar item.

What You'll Require

Tools / Equipment

- Crochet hook, US K/10.5 (6.5 mm)
- Coilless safety pins or stitch markers
- A yarn needle or a tapestry needle
- Scissors

Materials

- Worsted weight yarn (250-300 yards)

Instructions

1. Create a chain

Make a slip knot & put on the hook, leaving a six-inch tail of yarn; ch 15.

2. Work into Chain

In the 1st ch from your hook, place a stitch marker. [Ch 1, skipping upcoming ch, sc in upcoming ch] 6 times; turn. There will be 14 stitches total, with 7 sc stitches and 7 chain gaps (counting the space beside the highlighted stitch).

Tip

The turning chain was a stitch that is done in the middle of a row of crochet stitches. It elevates the piece's height from the ongoing row to the height required for the following row. It may be taken at the end of the row or at the beginning of a row in patterns. The start of a row may be identified in this design.

3. Establish a Foundation Row

Next Row: ch 1 (turning chains), [sc in next ch-1 sp & ch 1] 6 times, work sc into ch st at which marker was inserted, removing the marker before working the stitch. Turn around.

Tip

If you're having trouble locating your ch-1 spaces, gently poke the rows of stitches through the back to the front with your finger, exploring your ways into the work until you get the hang of recognizing where they are.

4. Begin with the Moss Stitch.

The remainder of the rows are identical to the previous row, with one slight

exception: at the conclusion of the row, work your final sc into the previous row's turning chain (tch).

All Rows: ch 1 (tch), [sc in next chain-1 sp, ch 1] 6 times, work a single crochet into turning chain.

Repeat this row until the scarf is about 50 inches long, or the desired length.

Finish:

Finish by fastening off, allowing enough yarn to weave in the ends. Use the end of the yarn, thread your tapestries needle & weave it into the design so that it is hidden. Repeat with any additional stray threads you may have. That's all there is to it; now put a crochet scarf around your neck & enjoy it.

4.2 Crochet Baby Blanket Pattern

Beginner skill, 300 minute

Who wouldn't want to make a quick and cuddly baby blanket with a free crocheted baby blanket pattern? Do you like fast tasks as much as we do?

You'll be able to finish this beauty in just 5 hours if you use thick yarn & a rapid stitch. This isn't your typical Moss stitch, however. Have you noticed the texture? This blanket was made using extended single crochet stitches, which you will really like.

Materials:

- Chenille yarn, size 6, very bulky. The example blanket was made using Bernat Blanket yarn in Dark Grey, Vintage White, & Bernat Baby Blanket in Shell Pink.
- Hook size N/P(10mm)
- To weave within ends, use a size K (6.5 mm) hook.

Finished Size

When placed flat, this piece measures 32 by 39 inches.

Yardage

Each of the three colors needs one skein. Each skein included 220 yards of yarn. Most of the cream hue was utilized, as well as 170 yards of grey and pink.

Abbreviations for Stitches

- ch-chain
- ch space stands for chain space.
- single crochet sc
- extended single crochet - esc
- beginning chain -beg ch

Explanations for Stitches

Put your hook into another st and draw up the loop, yarn over & draw through 1 loop, yarn over & pull through the other two loops on hook: 1 esc done

Gauge

5 esc stitches equal 5 inches

Ch 60, using the cream-colored yarn. To expand the breadth of your blanket, ch any even number.

Row 1: 1 sc in second ch from hook & each ch across (work this row tight). -59 sc

Row 2: Chain 3 (counts as an extended single crochet+ ch 1) skip next st, extended single crochet in next, *(chain 1, skip next st, extended single crochet in next), rep from * to end.

Row 3: Chain 3 (counts as an extended single crochet+ ch 1), sk the next st, extended single crochet in next, *(ch 1, skip next st, extended single crochet in next), rep from * to end.

Note: It can be found that putting your final st into the starting ch 1 created a straighter edge than working into the starting ch-2 at the finish of Row 3.

Row 4: Chain 3 (tallies as esc+ chain 1), sk the next st, 1 extended single crochet in next ch-space, *(chain 1, skip the next st, 1 esc in next chain-space), rep from * to last 2 sts (esc + beg ch), ch 1, skip next esc, 1 esc on top of starting ch-2, connect pink color yarn, fasten off cream color yarn.

Note: Rows 3 and 4 will be alternated with color changes in between.

Row 5: In color pink, repeat Row 3, joining color grey at the last of a row, & fasten off the pink. Turn around.

Row 6: In color grey, repeat Row 4, joining the color cream at the last of the row & fastening off the grey. Turn around.

Row 7: In color cream, repeat Row 3, joining color pink at the last of the row and fastening off the cream. Turn around.

Row 8: In color pink, repeat Row 4, joining color cream at the last of the row, & fasten off the pink. Turn around.

Row 9-23: In color cream, alternate Rows 3 and 4, joining color pink at the last of Row 23, & fastening off the color cream. Turn around.

Notes:

1. You may change the length of the blanket by crocheting more or less rows here, but be sure you keep track of the amount of rows for the next two panels.

2. From the top of a pink row, the cream panel measured roughly 9 1/2 inches.

Rows 24–38: Work in color pink for the following 15 rows, joining color grey at the completion of Row 38, then fasten off the pink. Turn around.

Row 55: In color cream, repeat Row 3, connect grey at the last of a row, & fasten off the color cream. Turn around.

Row 56: In color grey, repeat Row 4, connect pink at the last of the row, and fasten off color grey. Turn around.

Row 57: In color pink, repeat Row 3, joining cream at the last of the row and fastening off the pink. Turn around.

Rows 58-60: In color cream, repeat Rows 4, 3, and 4. Invert the situation.

Row 61: chain 2 (count as a hdc), 1 of hdc in each chain & st across to finish, fasten off.—-60 hdc

Note: Because the hdc makes the same size as the first colourful panel, the final row is an hdc row rather than a single crochet row from the first row.

Finishing

Weave in all the remaining tails using the smaller hook. To prevent your tails from displaying through the gaps, weave through the top half of your esc sts.

Row 39-53: For the following 15 rows, repeat Rows 3 & 4 in color grey, joining color pink at the bottom of Row 53, then fasten off the color grey. Turn around.

Row 54: In color pink, repeat Row 4, joining color cream at the bottom of the row and fastening off the color pink. Turn around.

4.3 Crochet Hat Pattern

Skill: Beginners, Time: 90 minutes

This crochet hat design for beginners is really simple, whether you simply need a fast project or new to crocheting. This basic unisex beanie design may be made by anybody who can crochet a rectangle.

To create a great tapered form, crocheting a hat typically requires a fair bit of counting when increasing or decreasing. This isn't the case. You'll use the most elementary crochet stitches to produce a gorgeously traditional ribbed beanie with this novel method. (Preemie through adult sizes)

Supplies:

- Wool-Ease Tonal Lion Brands – 2 skeins (Weight: 5 per bulky – 124 yards, 4 oz.) Smoke (635-149) & Slate Blue are the colors seen (635-107)
- Needle for tapestry
- Crochet hook, size L (8 millimeters)
- Safety pins or stitch markers
- Small piece of cardboard/ pom pom maker or fur pom pom

Dimensions:

S: Young adolescent (circumference of about 18" unstretched)

M: The majority of women and men (unstretched circumference: approx. 20")

L: Heads with a larger circumference (about 22" unstretched circumference)

Gauge:

4" = 10 stitches

4" = little over 4 rows

Glossary and Abbreviations (US Terms):

- ch (chain)
- dcblo - Double crochet via the back loop
- tch stands for "turning chain."
- sk – (skip)
- st - (stitch)
- RS stands for right side.
- WS stands for Wrong side
- rep – (repeat)

Notes on the Overall Pattern:

The pattern has been written in size S, with M & L in brackets. S (M/L)

Notes:

- A hat is crocheted in rows back and forth. These rows will produce the beanie's vertical ribs.
- The chain (Ch) 3 at the start of each row is not counted as a stitch.
- To make this crochet hat design fit a toddler, start with less stitches & work fewer total stitches.

- After Row 1, doubled crochet stitches are only crocheted beneath the back loop of the preceding row's thread. Regardless of whatever side of the crochet is facing you, this is the loop farthest distant from you.

Ch 37 foundation row.

Row 1: 1 dc in the fourth ch from hook & each chain (ch) to end of row; turn (34)

Row 2: Dcblo (double crochet through the back loop only) in each dc to the end of the row; turn (34)

Row 2 should be repeated 16 (18, 20) the most times for a maximum of 18 (20, 22) rows.

Leaving a 24 inches tail, fasten off.

The size of the rectangle should be approximate:

18" x 14.5'' (S)

20" x 14.5'' (M)

22" x 14.5'' (L)

Seaming Rectangle

Notes:

To calculate your fabric's RS and WS, do the following: Whenever the WS is facing, the tail of the last row must be on the left bottom if you're right-handed. If you're left-handed, the top left corner of your last row should have the WS facing you.

The seam is worked just via the chain stitches & the loop of each dc st closest to the seam to hide the junction.

With the WS facing up, lay the rectangle horizontally. If desired, use safety pins or stitch markers to pin the seam.

Tapestry needle having tail from fastening off threaded from both the top of the dc stitch, work into the top of the matching chain. Then, starting at the end of the following chain, work into the end of the adjacent dc. Carry on in this manner from the top of 1 dc to a top of 1 chain, then from the end of one chain to the bottom of 1 dc. Rep till the seam is finished.

Enter needle into crochet cloth to make a loop of yarn, now insert the needle into loop of yarn & pull tight to tie a basic sewing knot. This will avoid the puckering of the seam in the following step. Trim the yarn but do not cut it.

Top Closing

Whipstitch across the top of the hat using tapestry needle & strand of yarn leftover from the last seam, working 1 whip stitch through each row. Tighten the circles as much as possible, then stitch up any residual openings in the hat's top using a tapestry needle.

Adding a Pom Pom

Use a huge pom-pom machine or a 2.5" piece of cardboard to create a pom-pom. A gradual pom-pom technique may be found here.

How to create the pom-pom for a beanie in crochet or knit. The color "slate blue" is Lion Brands Wool-Ease Tonal yarn.

Sew pom pom fur or yarn to the hat using the tail left over from the seam.

Finish by tying off any loose ends and weaving them in.

Put the new crochet hat upon your head and start creating more for your friends and family.

4.4 Pattern for Crochet Slipper Sock

Supplies:

Made Easy Yarn Lion Brands Color, 54 to 157 yards or 1.52 to 4.44 Oz

Crochet Hook, Size K, 6.5 mm

Needle for yarn

A pair of scissors

Abbreviations and Stitches

- CH stands for the chain.
- SC stands for Single Crochet.
- DC stands for Double Crochet.
- SLST stands for Slip Stitch.
- ST(s) stands for Stitch (es)
- MC stands Magic Circle

Size & Gauge

2 inches = 3 Rows x 6 DC

By adding additional rows to the heel portion or toe, the length of a crochet slipper sock may be easily altered.

Notes:

- It's written in American terms.
- Your turning chain (chain 2) doesn't really count as the stitch.
- This design is designed for a toddler, with a kid and tiny women's size in brackets. When the patterns are done in the same way for all sizes, notes are provided.

Rows 1 & 2 are done in the same way regardless of size.

Toe Row 1: SLST to first DC, work 12 Double Crochet (DC) into a Magic Circle. (12)

Toe Row 2: Chain (CH2), *DC (direct crochet) into the next 03 STs, 02DC into the next ST* 3 times more. To the first DC, SLST. (Fifteenth)

Skip row 3 & continue on row 4 for the Toddler Size.

Toe Row 3: Chain (CH2), *DC into the next 4 Stitch (STs), 02DC into the next stitch* 3 times more. To the first DC, SLST. (18)

CH2, DC into following 15 (18, 18) Stitches (STs) on Toe Row 3(4, 4). To the first DC, SLST. (15, 17, 18, 19)

Row 3 should be repeated four times for the toddler size.

Rep row 4 a whole of the 5 times for the kid-size.

Rep row 4 a maximum of 7 times for the small women's size.

The toe section has been completed.

Heel of Slipper

You must have 6 rows completed for the size of toddler, 8 rows completed for the kid-size, and 10 rows completed for the small women's size at this point.

Heel Row 1: Chain 2, Dc into the next 12(15, 14) Stitches. (12, 15, 14)

Heel Row 2: Chain 2, turn, Dc into the next 12(15, 14) Stitches. (12, 15, 14)

Rep Heel Row 2 twice more for toddler size.

Rep Heel Row 2 three times for the kid-size.

Repeat Heel Row 2 four times for the small women's size.

The heel part is now complete.

Cuff for Slippers

We'll work 2 single crocheted into the side of every heel row for the slipper cuff, then single crocheted into the unworked stitch of Heel Row 1. Then, on the opposite side of the rows of heels, knit 2 single crochet.

Row 1 of the cuff: CH1, 2 SC in each of the following 3(4, 5) rows. Incorporate Single crochet (sc) into the following 3(3, 4) Stitches. In the following 3(4, 5) rows, work 2 single crochet (sc) into the side. To the first SC, SLST. (15, 19, 24)

Row 1 of the cuff is finished.

Cuff Row 2-3: CH2, DC on next 15 (19 to 24) Stitches. To the first DC, SLST.

Fasten off here for the toddler & kid sizes, leaving long yarn ends to stitch up the heel.

Cuff Row 4 (For Size, Small Women): CH2, Double Crochet (DC) into the next 24 Stitches. To the first DC, SLST. Finish with a longer yarn end to stitch up the heel.

Thread the yarn end onto a needle and weave it through the cuff row to the open heel to finish the crochet slipper socks. Sew up the heel using an invisible stitch or a whip stitch.

4.5 Market Bag Pattern

This basic crochet design creates trendy crochet market bags with plaid design or gingham using basic colorwork. This is a simple stash buster design that takes just one skein within each color. For a final touch, attach a ranch house rope handle or start crochet one's own.

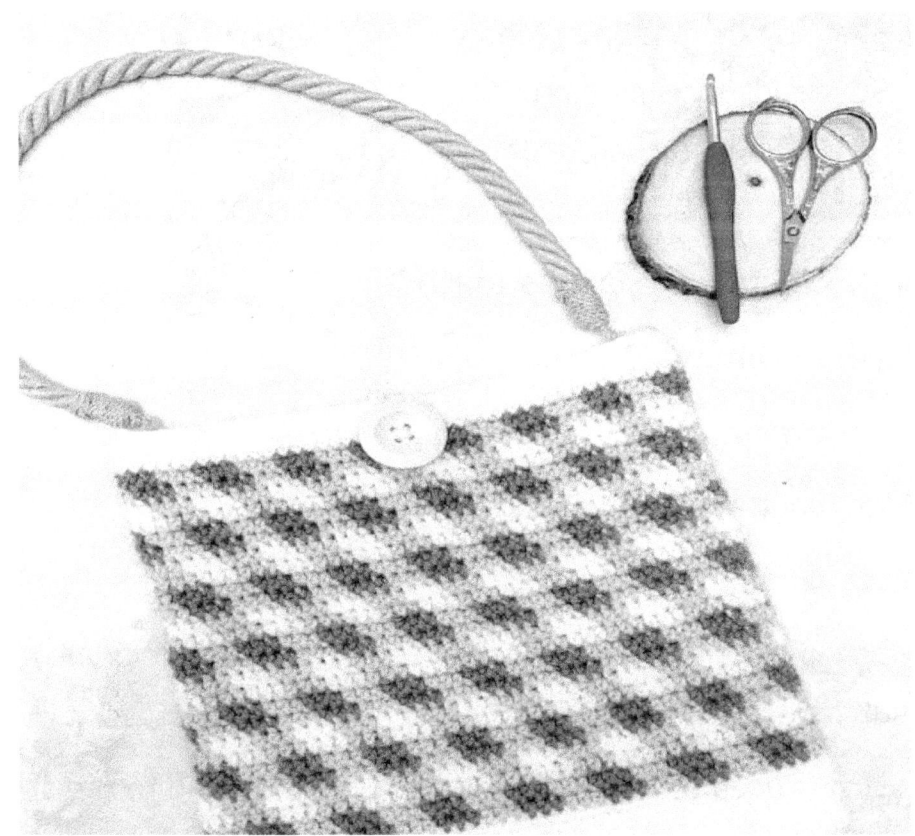

Supplies:

- Three colors of worsted weight yarn each color requires less than 170 yards. You can use Lion Brand Vanna's Choice & Loops & Threads Impeccable together.
- Crochet hook, H/5.0 mm
- Yarn Needle
- Scissors
- Handbag straps (one can easily get it from amazon)
- Button (1 1/2") (optional)

Abbreviations (in American terms):

- YO stands for yarn over.
- Ch stands for chain.

- Sl st stands for slip stitch.
- SC stands for single crochet.
- HDC stands for half double crochet.

Gauge

6-row x 9 sts = 2" squares In HDC,

Finished Dimensions:

10.5" in width

12" in length (without the strap).

Notes on the Pattern

The chain stitch at the start of each round does not qualify as a stitch.

An sl st is used to attach the ending of each round to the start stitch of the round.

Color A is white, Color B is light green, and Color C is dark green. The color green

We suggest carrying the yarn for color changes to reduce the number of endings to weave into it at the finish.

Begin with Color A.

Chain 44

Round 1: SC in the second chain (ch) from hook, Single Crochet (SC) in 41, 2 SC in the final chain (front side of ch). SC in 42, 2 Single Crochet (SC) in the final stitch on the rear (backside of chain) (this would be the 1st stitch you worked on the front). With an sl st, join the first single crochet (SC) of the round (88)

Round 2: (Chain) ch 1, *SC (single crochet) in 43, 2 SC (single crochet) in the next stitch, repeat from *, link with an sl st to the first SC (single crochet) of the round (90)

Rounds 3–10: Chain 1, SC all around, sl st to first SC (90)

Rounds 11-12 (Begin with Color B): (Chain) ch 1, *HDC into 3 stitches with Colors B, HDC in next 03 stitches with Color C, rep from * 14 times more. With an sl st, join to the 1st HDC of the round (90).

Rounds 13-14: ch 1, **HDC in first 3 stitches with Colors A, HDC into next 3 stitches with Colors B, rep from * 14 times more. With an sl st, join to the 1st HDC of the round (90).

Rounds 11-12 are repeated in Rounds 15-16.

Rounds 13-14 are repeated in Rounds 17-18.

Rounds 11-12 are repeated in rounds 19-20.

Rounds 13-14 are repeated in rounds 21-22.

Rounds 11-12 are repeated in rounds 23-24.

Repeat Rounds 13-14 in Rounds 25-26.

Rounds 11-12 are repeated in rounds 27-28.

Rounds 13-14 are repeated in Rounds 29-30.

Rounds 31-32 are the same as Rounds 11-12.

Rounds 13-14 are repeated in rounds 33-34.

Rounds 11-12 are repeated in rounds 35-36.

Rounds 37-39 (A Color): (Chain) ch 1, SC all around, sl st to first SC (90)

Round 40: (Chain) ch 1, SC in 20, Single crochet over handle loops for next 08 stitches, Single crochet in 37, Single crochet over handles loop for next 08 stitches, Single Crochet in 17, connect to first single crochet of the rounds with an sl st. Tight

Chain 10, skip 2 stitches & connect with an sl st to make a button loop.

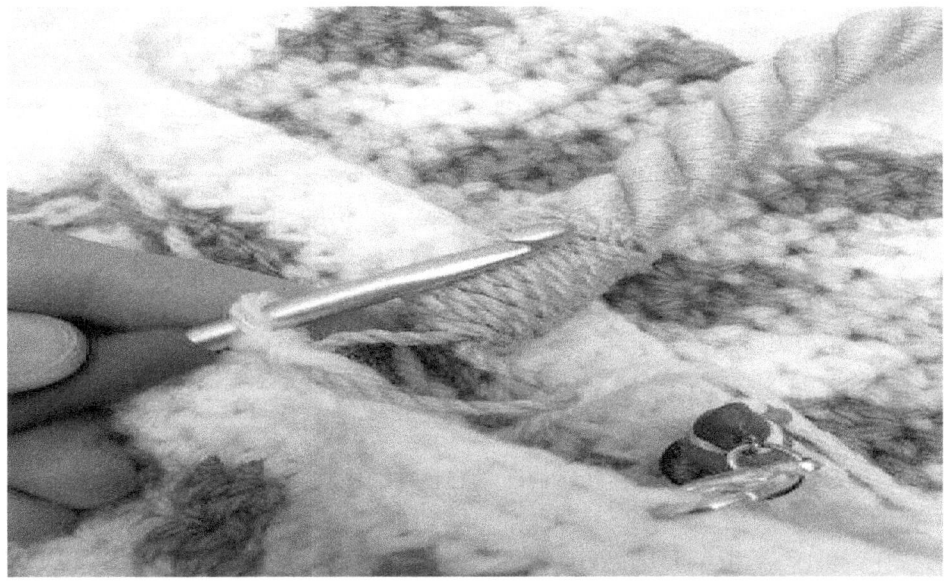

Note that the button loop is an optional feature. Finish the round of single crochet as normal if you don't want a button closing. Weave in all ends, Tie off yarn, and, if desired, attach a button.

Chapter 5: Wearing the Crochet

Antique doilies and old sweaters may come to mind when you think about crochet. Crochet tops, on the other hand, have made a comeback in a big manner. Crochet shirts come in a variety of styles, from large blouses to small crop tops, and are an essential part of any summer wardrobe. Learn which undergarments to wear along with crochet, what bottoms to match it with, as well as how to accessorize it flawlessly if you're adopting the trend.

5.1 Selecting Undergarments

1. Wear a tank top with no sleeves beneath. It might be difficult to choose a crochet top since they might look to be excessively exposed. Underneath your crochet top, a nude camisole is a right answer. It would not blend in or detract from the crochet design, which is the highlight of your ensemble if you choose a nude hue. You're also completely covered, so there's no need to be concerned about overexposure or seeming indecent.

2. Wear a bandeau or bralette beneath. You may choose not to cover yourself fully beneath your crochet top if you're feeling brave. Try putting it over a bandeau or a bralette instead. Bralettes are comparable to bras, however, they don't have underwire and don't seem as much like underwear as a standard bra. [2] Bandeaus are some kind of tube top that covers your chest with a strip of fabric. You could keep

your tummy visible in your crochet shirt while yet cover up your chest by wearing any of them beneath it.

Bralettes with all types of lovely details are available, & both bralettes & bandeaus are available in a number of colors. From under your crochet top, you may pick a lovely item to give interest to your ensemble.

3. Wear something bright beneath. You don't have to limit yourself to neutral tanks & underwear. In fact, a splash of color may be added to your look by wearing a royal blue tank top, a pink bra, or a bright scarlet bandeau beneath a crochet top. Make the rest of the outfit simple and allow the bright undergarment to draw attention to the top's design.

Try matching plain black shorts with such a black crochet shirt, but add a bright red camisole beneath for a splash of color.

By layering a neon color bandeau beneath jeans & a white crochet top, you may make the outfit more unique.

5.2 How to Wear a Crochet Top?

1. Wear your crochet shirt with a pair of jeans. Pair your crochet shirt with such a pair of jeans or shorts to keep the rest of your outfit casual. For a more informal, flower kid look, go for a tattered pair. Choose sleek and darker denim to spice up your look a little more. Jeans are a no-brainer since they work with every crochet top, regardless of style or color.

Wear a flowy, boho crochet top with holes and rips in your faded denim. This is a light and airy summer style. Wear a much more structured crochet shirt with a dark wash, cut jeans for a more formal look.

2. Use colourful, interesting designs in your crochet. With this suggestion, you may really embrace the hippy mood. Pair a solid-colored crocheted top with a vivid and eye-catching design on shorts, skirts, or trousers. Combining crochet with such a pattern is a much more daring option, and your ensemble will undoubtedly stand out.

Wear a flowery or paisley-patterned pair of shorts with a white crochet blouse. Wear a neutral-colored crochet blouse with a classic tie-dyed skirt.

3. Wear a maxi skirt for a bohemian style. It's really about balance if it comes to putting together a nice look. If you're wearing a little, sultry crochet blouse, balance out your look with a floor-length maxi skirt. The ideal bohemian garment is a lovely flowing maxi skirt. You may create a wonderful silhouette & strike the ideal mix between modest & risqué by matching it with a much form-fitting & exposing crochet top.

A miniskirt with a small crochet crop top may reveal more flesh than you like, while billowy skirts with a loose, floating crochet top may not produce the most complimentary silhouette.

Wear a high-waisted maxi with a cropped crochet shirt. You'll get a slim silhouette and show a little flesh without going overboard.

4. Pair it with a pair of dressy pants. Crochet may be worn without making you appear like you're going to a music festival or the beach. You may surely dress up your crochet shirt and wear it in a much more professional situation. It's all about equilibrium once again. Wear a more sophisticated pair of slacks or pencil skirt with your more informal crochet top. Combine an unstructured crocheted top with fitted pants to create a striking contrast.

It's ideal to combine your crochet top with a full-coverage tank top if you're wearing it to work.

Wear a tailored jacket over your crochet top to make it appear more professional.

5. Wear a monotone ensemble with your crochet shirt. Crochet is a great way to add interest to an outfit. Try layering a crochet shirt over a monochromatic outfit to add some interest. If you have a favorite black dress, experiment with adding a crochet layer to it. Try a multicolored crochet shirt over white slacks & a white tank top. You have a plethora of choices. In a monochromatic ensemble, a crochet shirt might be the ideal standout item.

5.3 Crochet Top Accessorizing

1. Wear some bright earrings. When it comes to crochet tops, the design usually has a lot going on. Chunky necklaces will draw attention away from the crochet, while small necklaces will blend in. Earring is one of the greatest ways to match it with jewelry. Pair exquisite, intricate crochet with much more delicate earrings, and bulky crochet tops with more simple earrings.

Rather of distracting from or contrasting with the crochet design, the earrings should complement it.

Wear a basic cream crochet shirt with flamboyant feather earrings, for example. Consider wearing something eye-catching, bright-colored earrings if your ensemble is monochromatic or more neutral.

2. Don a slouchy cardigan. A crochet shirt may not even be warm enough on colder days. Thankfully, these shirts look well with loose cardigans! Crochet shirts, especially those that are tighter or skimpier, look great with loose-fitting, easy sweaters. Find a cardigan that has the same weight & texture as the top and drape it loosely over your shoulders.

Wear a lightweight, flowy cardigan with a flowing crochet top. Cardigans that are thin yet large look great with crochet shirts.

3. Add some bangles to your ensemble. Nothing goes better with such a crocheted top than a wonderful bangle or

collection of bangles whenever it comes to bracelets. Because a crochet top's design is more organic & a solid, free-flowing, geometric bracelet contrasts wonderfully. Choose the simpler patterns; you won't need to add anything to these tops.

4. Match your crochet top with a handbag or bag. Instead of opting for an extremely structured, hefty handbag, go for a lighter, unstructured version. Fringed or floral-print bags will go well with the boho aesthetic. Lightweight cross-body bags can store all of your belongings while being casual and unobtrusive.

Chapter 6: Crochet Gifts & Home Decor

Crocheting is increasingly becoming a popular pastime among many people. Even if you're new to knitting, there are a plethora of delightfully simple designs to choose from. In actuality, there are a few items that you may start crocheting right now and complete before the ending of the day. To share with you, I've gathered 30 of my favorite beginning crochet designs. These items would also make great presents, so if you're in a hurry and need a present, grab your crochet hooks & get started.

We have to confess that we like getting homemade presents, and we are ready to wager that we are not alone. One can be assured that there is a pattern that will help you choose a present for anybody. Most of them take an hour or less to complete, making them fast presents that are also simple to crochet. This crochet for the beginner's book also includes a lot of fantastic gift ideas. They're also simple patterns and tasks that may usually be completed in an hour or less.

Patterns for beginners are essential while learning how to crochet. They're simple to read, and you'll be able to practice and master fundamental stitches before going on to more difficult designs. Of obviously, you would like to learn much more than single crochet, and therefore this collection includes designs that employ a variety of stitches — they're all simple to learn, but you won't be trapped repeating the same stitch in each one. They're also ideal for people who have learned crochet and are looking for quick and simple present ideas.

The following are some items that can be crocheted in less than an hour and given as gifts or used to decorate one's house. It's crucial to note that these are merely names; instructions for making them may be found in the chapter of the project.

- Beautiful Crochet Gloves
- Delicate Shoes for Toddlers
- Crochet Cardigan
- Crochet Hexagon Sweater
- Pineapple Crochet Hat
- Crochet Potholder
- Crochet Mitten
- Crochet Hand Bags
- Crochet Socks & Slippers
- Crochet Curtains, Rags & Baskets for Home Décor
- Crochet Wall Hangings
- Crochet Ornaments

You can easily give all these items as gifts to your loved ones and if you have gone through this book you will be able to do it on your own within no time. So wait no more time and start crocheting right now.

Conclusion

This book is appropriate for all crocheters, including those with little prior experience and those with very advanced capabilities. If you've never used a crochet hook earlier but would like to learn, the book will walk you through all of the fundamental stitches so you can produce stunning tiny and big objects. If you also know well how to crochet, there is a tremendous choice of unusual and lovely designs to try out at a reasonable price.

Crochet takes you through the fundamental stitches and methods, presenting them clearly & simply with step-by-step images and explaining the abbreviations and symbols along the way. Beginners may work their way through the book's first portions thorough and easy-to-follow methods section, pausing along with the attempt to stimulate out such a tiny item to practice the stitch they've just learned. This book may also be used by more experienced crocheters to review stitches they already know. From basic chains stitch bracelets to a beautiful intarsia cushion, the little crafts are diverse. Once you've mastered all of the crochet stitches, go on to the crafts section and start crocheting things like a classic granny blanket for a newborn, a little sock for a toddler, & small girl's market bag.

There's something for everyone with over 80 projects to pick from, including blankets and pillows, hats and scarves, gloves, socks, and slippers, household goods, clothing and bags, and a variety of lovely toys to create. Crochet allows you to create one-of-a-kind crocheted items for your home, yourself, and your family & friends.

www.ingramcontent.com/pod-product-compliance
Lightning Source LLC
Chambersburg PA
CBHW081421080526
44589CB00016B/2624